THE
HISTORY
OF
INTIMACY

THE HISTORY OF INTIMACY

POEMS

GABEBA BADEROON

TriQuarterly Books / Northwestern University Press
Evanston, Illinois

TriQuarterly Books
Northwestern University Press
www.nupress.northwestern.edu

Printed in the United States of America

10   9   8   7   6   5   4   3   2   1

Library of Congress Cataloging-in-Publication Data

Names: Baderoon, Gabeba, author.
Title: History of intimacy : poems / Gabeba Baderoon.
Description: Evanston, Illinois : TriQuarterly Books/Northwestern University Press, 2021.
Identifiers: LCCN 2021000844 | ISBN 9780810143609 (paperback)
Subjects: LCGFT: Poetry.
Classification: LCC PR9369.4.B33 H57 2021 | DDC 821/.92—dc23
LC record available at https://lccn.loc.gov/2021000844

To my mother—
groundbreaker, healer, muse

CONTENTS

POETRY FOR BEGINNERS

In the evening poetry class for beginners
a girl in a thick brown coat she doesn't take off

breathes in deep
and risking something says fast

my boyfriend's in prison

I'm here to find out
how to write to him through the bars

and someone laughs

and she pulls herself back into her coat
and from inside looks past us

and the next week
doesn't come back

and I think of her for years
and what poetry is

I think this is my origin
where poetry is risk, is betrayal

and the memory of the first question
how not to be alone

TELL ME WHAT YOU SEE

In the small caravan parked permanently next to the Traffic Department
with the handwritten sign *ID Photos Taken Here*
its wheels rusted into place
the young old photographer with dreadlocks and a tired poet's face
is shaking his head from side to side
muttering some version of no
what kind of photographer are you asks a woman ahead of me
you don't make the people smile
I just do my job lady and then I get out of here
you would also be like this if you worked here
no you mustn't let them change you my boy
I would still be smiling
ja maybe for the first two months
but then they'll drive you crazy
just before me in the caravan
a woman in a long black skirt and black veil unties
the loop of fabric knotted at the back of her head
and her face briefly emerges
the young old photographer sees everything
hundreds of unclaimed photos line the inside of his caravan
the making of identity interrupted
and turned into small sad signs
of something else
we don't look at each other so we look
at the walls
at the faces
no one came to collect
someone stands and someone offers their seat
exact change
I sit on the plastic barstool
and he takes my picture with a small digital camera
like the one you take holiday photos with
no tripod except his legs and arms

the background behind me
the faded fawn of the caravan wall
that disappears anyway in the end
why do we all hate our ID photos
our faces without spectacles hair tucked
behind the ears eyes too wide the moment
our identity, identity is being made
the photographer runs a small HP photoprinter
on a car battery humming constantly
like the queues and the questions and the promises
of whatever keeps this government building working
in the hall with its rows of plastic chairs
a man ahead of me presses his finger onto the ink blotter
a thousand index fingers before him
then he leans his forehead against the eye-test machine
tell me what you see the officer says
to clean the ink from his thumb
she gives him a single square of toilet paper
torn carefully at the perforated line
in the last queue to pay for my temporary license I slide
four photos my ID book completed form and exact change
into the metal slot under the glass
ma'am put your left thumb on the inkpad
and place it inside the block
she watches me sign
in the right place and pastes
a strip of sellotape over my name fixing
my identity for six months at least

CLOSER

I used to live in a small room
with a narrow bed
and a television at my feet.
A mirror hung
on the back of the door.
I lived in the order
of its smallness.

I lie here next to you
and feel the distance
from the walls.
If I held you closer
we would fit
on a narrow bed.

A PROSPECT OF BEAUTY

I walk down Heerengracht,
where pigeons dip their necks
like question marks into the fountain.
Then right at Riebeeck and into Loop

while the sun slips into the sea
and the moon takes its place over Signal Hill.
Above me, starlings clatter
like typewriters.

Higher still, turning right at Wale,
seagulls tilt like white kites
against the wind.

I pass through the old silences of the city.

Here is the place on the hill
where artists sought quiet
and the view of the harbor.
Below, the city reveals itself.

We still walk the neat streets
as though inside their paintings.

Under the angled mountain, the soft light,
the starlings are cold, and I cannot look away
from their chaotic and coordinated hunger.

What can explain
this exact and unjust beauty?

The flock clusters at sunset for warmth and seed.
Poetry cannot be afraid of this.

Sketching the streets, the artists stood
on the burial ground of the city's slaves.
In the paintings is something
of the private grief of their fettered bodies.

In precise patterns, the starlings shadow each other
and double back on their own flight paths,
slipstreams of warmth,
blood-trace of the self.

Nothing to begin with,
and nothing again.

Around me, the air thickens with history.
On this day two hundred years ago,
slaves could no longer be sold.

Nothing, and nothing again.

I look once more at the painted streets, falling
silent at sunset, even the birds stilled.
In the last flash of the sun, the city glints
white and hard as bone.

SURFACE

One day in the nineties
we sat around talking after a conference
in the mountains and a white boy asked us
to make names for the colors of our skin,
a conversation we could only have
far from where we lived
in the separate parts of the city.
We were hungry for something,
not quite this, but still,
our wanting made us risk it.

Joburg Cinnamon, a girl declared to begin,
and she was
the burnt-sweet bark of a tree
cleaved into history.
Athlone Coffee, I offered, not revealing
Ricoffy, the cheap instant we used in our house,
one spoon tapped level
against the rim of the bowl, condense milk
not quite mixed in, eddies
inside the dark making
the color of my hand as I stirred.

South African white, he claimed, a finger to his chest,
then, pointing to a thinner boy, *real* white,
a confession of beginnings
made out of skin,
what he wanted to say from the start.
It was the first time I admitted to myself
I loved the skin of white boys.
Him I kissed with my eyes closed
in someone else's bed, a brittle pleasure
brief as breath.

And another, who, driving a friend home,
reached past the edge of the seat for my hand
and we closed our fingers around each other,
hungry, hidden, biding
our time till the end.

Does it matter there were no names
for whiteness
but the whole
and the real,
back when we tried and failed
to make a new country?
I see now I always wanted
what was furthest from me, a boundary
I conjured into flesh
that disappeared beneath my fingers.
I never resolved
the mess of it, the way
want is desire
and lack at the same time.

When I opened my eyes, I told him,
Bite my shoulder, watching
his face as I said it, Yes, hard,
into his eyes, wanting
a little of the hurt
to come to the surface and stop.

THE FLATS

In the city the yellow cranes pause mid-swing
and the scaffold lattice clanks hollow in the wind.
Under the Civic Centre, a column of silence
and shadow divides the street.

Thirty years ago, my father in his white hard hat stood
on a platform outside a building he helped raise
to the sky, his back to the impervious glass,
staring at something I cannot see.

Their suburb was declared white
in the year he and my mother married
and they were removed
to a place you cannot trace from here.

I was born on the Flats,
with its sand streets and damp walls,
a winter child, a child of loss.

Each day the route to work took them
past their old house, brought them close again
to what they had lost,
and they never looked in its direction.

Born in the new place, I was their ghost child,
a grief growing
older and older.

On days like this, I forgive them
what they could bear to look at
and what they could not.

I forgive them their slow love
of the new place,
of me.

They turned distance into an ordinary tragedy
and eventually a home.

Without them,
the city falls silent each day.

PORT JACKSON, CAPE TOWN

Alien wattle, quick-growing
firewood of the poor, bitter smoke
that reddens the sunsets.

In wattle fields, twenty boys lie
and women weep each year
on the day and the hour
their sons disappeared.

GREEN PINCUSHION PROTEAS

Green pincushion proteas grow
in my mind, swaying faintly
in today's wind. Memory snagged me
through the pink pincushions I bought this morning
from the auntie in the doek by the Kwikspar,

who added a king protea to the bunch,
all spikes and pins in reds and maroons,
so regal that as a child I didn't know
it was alive
and did not water it.

My mother's remembering
remembers them into me.

Do you remember, she asks, so I do,
green pincushion proteas this small?
Her fingers slowly bloom
flowers the size of large coins
we found here among the stones and sand.

Do you remember, she asks,
and the green coins bud into the first bush
long preceding us. All tangles
and snaggings and swayings,
green pincushions prick into my mind,
thicken themselves stitch by stitch
into a place that is again.

Now fervent with color, green blooms clamber
over the rockery, but careless we,
who did not know their beginnings, wrench them
from their original rocks and move them
to another part of the garden.
They died, she recalls.
They don't like their roots to be moved.

So they withdrew a little
and then fully, gone
even from memory until now,
a species of green, blossoming and unmoved.
Why did we move them to another place,
we, who were removed to here?
Do you remember, she asks.

BLACK BUTTERFLIES

On the morning walk at Silvermine,
trees are black lace against the sky.
At our knees, hinged silhouettes
flicker free of each other,
shadows of shadows,
doubled half-circles, fluttering
like fragments of midnight
to our feet, then rising again.

GHOST TECHNOLOGIES

On button. Red light we learn the meaning of.

In 1976 the Soweto student protests are erased from the black-and-white television that arrives that year in the front room and from then on a line is drawn between what happened and did not, what is real and is not.

Each night, we children eat hurriedly in the next room, our eyes already sidling through the door to the blank screen. Just before six, waiting on chairs facing the new center, we watch an intuition pulse through black-and-white snow. It flickers, then hisses and turns into the high whine of the test pattern, that on the dot of six becomes a face.

Prayer starts the evening as prayer will end it at midnight with the Epilogue.

The continuity announcer's lips slide suddenly into sidelong fractions till we jiggle the bunny aerial and prop it upside down on the mantel behind the screen.

My parents make a timetable. No watching after the eight o'clock news, so *after the news* becomes a genre for grown-ups. No TV on Sundays, when the state teaches you to become Christian.

Telefunken, Fuchsware, Tedelex—the names next to the *On* button change as our TVs break over the years. The single channel alternates between English and Afrikaans, then the government creates new stations in Zulu and Xhosa. We are trained into separate realities.

The first time I see a Black woman on TV is in an advert for dishwashing liquid in which a white woman praises her domestic servant for choosing a new detergent. "Betsy, you're so clever," to which the Black woman responds shyly, "Oh, madam." Even as a child, I can see this is not about cleaning plates but some other kind of labor.

We watch to become ourselves.

TV teaches us good Black voices. The Black people reading the news sound as though they are sitting inside glass, and come from nowhere we know.

In 1982 my mother buys a Philips videocassette recorder with a semi-remote control at the Rand Easter Show and one day someone trips over the twelve-foot cord and after that the VCR only works with the cord plugged in.

In *Live and Let Die*, my eyes widen when James Bond has sex with Rosie Carver, a desire apartheid seemed to make almost biologically impossible. I press rewind on the semi-remote and watch again.

My brother buys an Apple computer with a green screen and orange cursor he hooks up to the TV. We play tennis and the ball sounds urgent but hollow, our fingers sore from slamming the arrow keys, the beginning of games that hurt and where only the screen makes a sound.

In the early days of the internet I navigate with arrow keys and DOS and in 1994 choose my first email name: *gab*. Messages sent to it still reach me today. In 2002 I move for a year to England, the center of the real, and have to queue in person at the bank because their online world seems not to exist. Down here, we rejig every technology and accelerate the virtual in the absence of the physical.

But capital is watching and tells us airtime is oxygen, a perfect philosophy of the real. In our houses, ghost technologies run down the prepaid electric meters.

Precise injuries of the neck, thumb, and eye create a new kind of body. The machines we hold close prompt infinite new desires and an infinite hunger for newness.

We don't notice when the category of *evening* disappears—the word for *after 5*, an *Off* button that once brought work to a close.

KOGELBAAI

Carrying our green canvas tents—darned
and patched after thirty years of camping—
down the mountain at Kogelbaai, we passed
the ghosts my uncle saw.

After the children fell asleep on the gudri-
padded ground, he told my brother late at night
stories of the wraiths of slaves who crossed
the mountains two centuries ago and are still hiding.

Born with the helm, he learned after his early terror
not to open his mouth lightly,
but to look through the door of time
and see when the mountain was the steep route of escape.

And how they disappeared into the kloof
barely eating and keeping one another alive
and still do.

Tell us ghost stories, we children said,
but he shook his head, a shadow himself,
and made a joke, his voice tapering off.

PROMISED LAND

Bird cry in the keys,
gliding to a low ending.
Hummingbird fingers quiver,
dip, and still
a note to almost nothing,
then you begin again,
training my heartbeat
to follow.

I listen to you at night
when I'm lonely
and not sure anymore.
So old at eighteen, you and not-you
led us to where stillness trembles
into rapture, and rapture
into knowing we exist,
even if existence is thin
as breath.

I hear your breath in the notes,
silence an inflection
running through everything.
Your father played you Monk
like he was family
and your grandfather gave you marabi,
so you came from a long line
before the future opened
in you. Even then
you looked back
like the angel of history, raising
your wings into the yet-to-come,
but facing the direction you had left.

Sixteen years ago, yours
was the CD I packed in my suitcase
to tell without words
where I'm from,
not just the music
but the new, intricate country
we understood
was impossible.

In those years of promises, you rested
in no easy melodies but composed
the difficult and searching dimensions
of the almost-world.
Your playing took us near beauty
because it might be enough
but in the end never is,
so you led us instead to the mapless place
of our longing.

The millennium ended after one year
with your death, presaging
our other losses.
Now I've lived past my youth
and also the silences I kept back then.

Moses, why
even today do we barely speak
of Florence,
who made the music happen,
and last,
and lay at your feet that night,
no words anymore between you?
But hers were the first to stop.

Even here,
she is at the end of the story,
her voice stilled.
Unsolved, they say,
but is it because
we've agreed not to ask?

All these years I've trembled at the door
between language and music, trying
the hinge between two beginnings,
and did my longing also hide her
from my mind?
Was her silence
the price of yours?

Our forgetting is also
our home, and why
we never left the old country.
Now it is the after
and I've grown into the questions.
Listening in the dark,
I'm lonely and not sure anymore.

NO NAME

My parents only bought in bulk or on discount, No Name brands. They
saved up for years, saying no to all our requests, then bought everything in
cash, even the car. Eventually we learned not to ask for things, not even to
want them. Even desire was pared from us.

Our salt was No Name. Our milk. Our clothes. Ourselves. In those plain
white boxes with blue writing, the label of No Money fell on us, stuck to our
skin, told us that we ourselves were generic, interchangeable. No Name was
clear on our bodies. To not matter at the level of skin was the law, but to not
matter at the level of what we wore and ate—that cut deeper than law.

Now after all those decades of discipline, something is loosening, being
overwritten by the body, by the present. My mother grumbles about a spoon
or doek she cannot find in the endless maelstrom of the house and I try to
salve the loss by repeating something I've heard from her all my life, Daai is
maar doenya se goete—These are only earthly things.

But I am on the earth, she replies, suddenly unanswerable. Yes, she is on
the earth and Parkinson's has given her permission to turn to what has been
refused, deferred, forbidden, not-now.

Not. Non. Non-white. The power of that negative, that emptiness, against
the fullness of white. Non. No. During apartheid, we created a potent No
of our own in order to resist, to struggle. We understood that to withdraw
ourselves, to disappear deliberately, to call attention to our absence, would
make our Non matter. If we don't exist for you, we bargained, how does it feel
when our money, our labor, our presence doesn't? Our potent Nos grew and
boycotts cut against the Non and against the nonexistence of us. We screamed
against the blank, the No Name. We refused, we said No to the Non.

But it was not Yes. A No against Non is not Yes. It was still raging against,
and on the other side was fullness, desire, Yes. To us who had been made into
fractions, into nothing, into not-on-this-earth, "Black" offered a new home,

a fullness. And yet it was a public fullness, a fullness for the era of privation. We had No, we had boycotts, we withdrew into our complex silences and absence, but behind them was a private hurt, the hurt of the Non. And so upon freedom, No did not protect us from a certain emptiness.

When freedom came, we thought our public fullness was enough; we thought we were ready for the pell-mell factories of desire and debt. We learned to speak ever finer and finer languages of existence, and we felt in our blood, in our bones, in our being, that existence lay in labels, in brands, in names. We rejected homemade food for restaurant buffets and wines with mythical price tags. We shuddered from the shame of rough hems sewn by our mothers after work and discarded them for the machine-made, even in my house where my father was a tailor and my mother worked for the unions and we could recite facts about labor conditions and open borders and product dumping and job losses. But what we knew consciously was nothing to what we knew in our skin.

In the old days I would walk into a shop in Cavendish Square, two streets from the house in Ingle Road that my family was removed from, and already by the way I inhabited my body, I showed that I didn't belong there. I was No Name. Now I can walk up to the shop assistant and hand her what I desire and pay for it, go into debt for it and know that this is mine, this is me. I am not generic. Not No Name. Not nothing.

Don't tell me that the small hurts don't matter, that our private emptiness doesn't count. Every label visible on the outside of the garment is a scream against Non. In freedom we wear brands on our skin until we believe what they say, until no one can tell by our clothes who exists and who does not. We buy our existence. Our bodies clothed in labels, we ourselves become brands. At last we are not nothing, we exist, we are a name.

On this earth. I am on this earth.

FOCAL LENGTH

I take out the black-and-white photos
I carried with me to this country
and haven't looked at for years
and place them next to one another
on the dining room table.

In one, my mother is young, standing
by the window, holding the telephone
with its spiraling black cord to her ear,
the curtain slanting to the side
as she turns toward the camera.

When I unwrapped them, the tissue paper
had only one set of creases, untouched
since she packed them for their long journey.

In the soft focus of faded paper, I am on her lap,
leaning against her like gravity.
She is looking at me, like my father
who is taking the picture.

My face is clear and hers slightly blurred,
as though his eyes are moving between us,
as though the camera cannot capture
the eye's oscillation between two people
one loves at the same time.

Another photo had been folded into three,
bent once and then again to fit into a pocket,
close enough to the skin to warm the paper,
then smoothed out again to fit into the wooden frame.

In it, I am turning sideways toward the camera
—someone must have called my name—
and a line creases just beneath my eyes.

Folded, hidden, forgotten,
memory doesn't come to me straight.
The pleat of the curtain as she leans against it,
the paper keeping its original fold,
me turning toward my name.

THE EDGES OF THINGS

Evening's soft forgiveness of the edges of things,
budding purple birches, yellow willows,
a still figure lingering on the margins.

Waiting fox, where are you going?
I hope back on the path behind you.
Nothing here is worth the crossing.

Stay there, recede.
You might never have been.

I am glad you broke cover,

but go back, vanish
into private lanes
only you know.

Leave me longing
at this point on Route 84
we were both passing
and may never see again.

STONE SKIN

In the castle, the statues stiffen
with perfection. Outside the stone walls,
the Malian immigrants stretch out their hands
full of roses and good fortune.

The boy lays his small foot on marble,
light and eternal. The Madonna holds his head
on her lap. Outside, the gestures of the hands
are not aesthetic, are not silent.

At night, the stone wall keeps in its place
and outside, the silence, the growing silence.

THE RIVER CITIES

This is the spine. This is what you face
or turn your back to, point of origin
or destination in the city.

Keening seagulls over the harbor,
the starting whine of an engine, slap
of waves on wood and metal, the sap
and throb of the tide.

In the evening, lights flick on in the water
pulsing against the dockside offices.
The sky above the river, mirror
of the bridge-span in the water,
busies with light.

Lines of flight, telephone lines, lightning
crosshatch the air, electric
as the ground, as under the ground.

Between the river cities, Antwerp and London,
the train windows look out on green fields
and a VW factory with its stalled cars
waiting to leave, like the parking lots
of Uitenhage, union town of my birth.

The train glides past a power station
pinch-waisted as an hourglass, coughing
silently into the air like its twin used to do
down the street from my mother in Athlone.

For two and a half hours, time
and countries go by.

Twenty minutes from London, the buildings begin again.
Brown- and red-brick houses pack close together,
their unpainted back walls and private gardens
briefly vulnerable to our eyes.

Remnants of green crowd the sides
of office blocks, but the city takes hold.
Now the river runs up to the train tracks
on one side and then under.

We slide into the bright veins of tunnels
under the Schelde, the Channel, the Thames.
In the dark our passage is marked off
in bright spokes of neon. Then day again,
and tall insurance buildings, schools,
and the graffitied walls of the station.

But in the tunnels, the unwatched run silently
alongside the trains or cleave
to the underside of the carriage,
not moving.

RAIN FALLS ON THE ABSTRACT WORLD

—after a print by Frans Masereel

Rain falls
until nothing is itself.

Rain falls
on the stones, on the night.

Rain falls through the gleam of the streetlight
and on its long shadow.

Rain slants
its angles steeper than the roofs.

Rain falls on the doorways
and on vacant thresholds.

Rain falls
on the loneliness of the world.

CONCENTRATION

Ahead of me
a man and a woman walk slowly
holding each other's waist,
no space between them.
Without warning, they stop.

I can't tell if they are talking.
He looks thin; her hip is a little behind his.
Then they walk quickly toward their door,
as though they have used up all their time.

Two doors from them, a man with a graying beard
smokes a cigarette, watching the couple.
This is his house, his hand
against the frame declares.
When they step inside,
he throws down the cigarette
and grinds it out with his shoe.

Three doors down, a woman in a black scarf
taps softly, softly against a white door.
She faces the impervious threshold,
not wanting to be looked at.
This is what her body says,
Do not look at my solitude.

Then I am at my own doorway,
remembering to turn the lock twice.
There are so many of them here,
my landlady confides,
a concentration.
It's not good.

This is the future,
these closing
and opening doors.

EVERYTHING WE'VE SAID[*]

English can only be a beautiful language
if we remember everything
we've said in it.

Afrikaans kan net 'n pragtige taal wees
as ons alles onthou
wat ons daarin gesê het.

لا يمكن أن تكون اللغة العربية لغة جميلة
إلّا إذا تذكّرنا كلّ ما
قد قلناه فيها

Deutsch kann nur eine schöne Sprache sein
wenn wir uns an alles erinnern
was wir darin gesagt haben.

IsiXhosa sinokuba lulwimi oluhle
kuphela ukuba sihlala sikukhumbula konke
esithe sakuthetha sisebenzisa sona.

Le français peut être une belle langue seulement
Si nous nous rappelons tout
Ce que nous avons dit en elle.

---

* While studying the languages above, I frequently heard the same point made about
each of them: Oh, ___ is such a beautiful language.

THE BLUE OF THE NIGHT BEFORE WE LEFT

Seagulls white against white stone buildings
and a painted ceiling of blue sky.

Stillness at dusk so we hear their wings beat
against the undersides of their bodies.

We lose ourselves without loss
in tessellated streets and the darkening hours.

The blue is the blue of late evening,
the blue of the night before we left.

In the city's architecture of nightfall,
marble statues soften into other densities.

Gulls wheel around columns of pitted stone,
their liquid cries floating above our leaving.

SONG OF THE HUSBAND 2

The nurse swathes your face and hands
in cotton against hard edges
for the long drive by ambulance to the big hospital
to keep your heart beating.

I turn off the radio to concentrate
on following at the right distance,
not distracted by music.

I look if possible inside the white van,
its lights not on, and see your head in white bands,
held softly in place. I test the straps
that hold you still on the mountain route.

How high the roads are here, I see,
till I am not on Earth anymore
but driving toward my destiny,
you a constant

and irretrievable distance ahead of me,
slipping out of my hands,
already held by some waiting fate,
gently and without answers.

EFFECTIVE IMMEDIATELY

Effective immediately,
there will be no visitor traffic into or out of the institution
between the hours of 12:30 and 1:15 P.M.
Please plan accordingly.

Visitors and inmates will sit straight, facing forward.
No arms around each other.
No sitting on laps.
No placing legs on tables or chairs.
No sitting sideways. No touching.

Hugging and greeting is only allowed
when first meeting and upon departure.

Children are crying.

Inmates are not permitted to use the vending machines.
Inmates are not permitted to handle money at any time.

I ask the guard for something to write on and she directs me to a cupboard
with boxes of plain white paper and blunt pencils. The whole cupboard
shakes as I turn a yellow stub in the old-fashioned sharpener screwed into
the edge of the shelf. The nib stays broken and I go back for another nub
to write with.

Inside.

He tells us about Code Z for "predators and prey." I say, Sorry, I didn't catch
that, and immediately wish I hadn't when he leans forward in his brown suit
with orange trim and soft-soled white shoes and explains, his mother next
to us, that "Code Z" means those who have attacked other people, or have
been raped, his trimmed white beard marking thirty-one years since he first
entered here.

He doesn't tell us he's been on the honor block for twenty years.

We talk about Kurosawa films, prison reform, and the book about African aid by Dambisa Moyo.

Effective immediately.

All coats and jackets will be hung on the coatrack.

All metals except gold rings, earrings, and necklaces must be removed.

He says, They can take it away from you at any time.

No tobacco products of any kind are permitted inside.

His mother tells us matter-of-factly, as though the sadness of it disappeared a long time ago, you can't get too close to other families. They could be police informers and tell the guards something the prisoner has told you. Everyone is desperate to get out of here.

Hours later, I try to cut off the blue armband around my wrist that says I do not belong behind the heavy steel doors, the bars, the 5,000 lights, the laser beams covering the grass and open spaces, the fences, the knocking on the cell walls twice a day to check for I-don't-know-what. My scissors are useless and after showering with the armband on, I tear it off in pieces.

Twenty years and they can take it from you at any time.

When I look online for blogs about the prison, I see posts written at 4 A.M., 4:02, 4:06.

CELL PHONES, PAGERS, and CAMERAS are prohibited and should remain in the vehicle.

I think of the nub of pencil.

Visitors are not permitted to leave anything, including gifts, money orders, etc. for the inmate. No objects may be exchanged between a visitor and an inmate.

All visitors (including minors) are required to pass through a walk-through metal detector. Please dress accordingly.

From the blogs I see this means no underwire bras, no metal in belts, no steel bangles.

Visitors must sign in upon arrival and sign out before leaving. All information requested on the sign-in sheet, including names and complete addresses, must be filled in completely. If you travel by private vehicle, you will be asked to register the year, make, model, and license number of the vehicle.

I always forget my license number and invent one each time.

He used to love to eat the food she brought him on Christmas, but one year the governor got tough on crime and put an end to all that. He teaches other prisoners to take their high school diplomas. He learned Spanish. He referees weekend basketball games. He does yoga for two hours each morning. He calls home every Saturday. He only reads nonfiction—What use is narrative?—and shares his books with two other longtimers. It costs him more to phone his mother than for me to call overseas. Prisoners have to call collect and she always accepts.

Food items, snacks, and beverages may be purchased from the vending machines located in the visiting areas.

The machine trembles when I touch it.

DIVING

Crossing the tea-dark water of the river pool,
my body recognized
its element and wanted to stay.

Cradled in my skull,
floating in its own ocean,
I felt the thin bone between me and me.

So I crossed slowly, ready
never to leave.

All this came back thirty feet under
the jetty where we practiced
after the pool and suddenly

breathing became strange, inward swell
of lung, outward jolt,
rhythm wouldn't beat
and repeat, each step
a fresh volition, reflex battling
with training, remember,
pull in air, not too fast
or much.

Panic has its own form,
too quick, too deep, its blue too opaque,
fish through which the waves pulse, rise
in a school whole, too much, too much
wonder and alien softness.

If I can stop dying, I can see
the water and light make peace
here where I do not belong
but remember

AXIS AND REVOLUTION

Glass door in a glass wall,
screen of reflections, rain-
streaks, fingerprints, slips
the catch of the lock, swings

slowly open, axis and revolution,
reflecting a compass of sky,
trees, the sun in rain, windows
of the houses opposite, me watching.
Flashing glass on glass, the door fans
its cards of mirrors.

In the door, I am a reflection
on reflections, gleaming
against the facing windows, seamless
turning, turning

outside into inside, opening
a dark glint of entry to your house.
Through glass skin,
I am inside, invited in.

Stiff glass sail catches
a sudden clip of wind, gathers
speed to whip wide
toward a tipping point,
its own reflection, the end
of its half-circle,
glass door against glass wall.

Across the road, behind my own reflections,
I am too far to run and catch
the door before it reaches

the end of its span, slams
backward against glass.

Stretching its hinge, the door scrapes
the clear wall only briefly, then springs back,
shuddering, ringing, heading
home to the lock again,

or right through, cracking and splaying
on impact, hurtling across the threshold,
past the curtains, into the rooms.

Search as you will, you'll never find
all of me. Some splinter
of light will elude you, stay.

Did I see your hand reach
the door in time, click it fast?

Fastened, sealed, glass door giving
back what it keeps outside.

THE PORT CITIES

The city turns its back
on the river, its first circle.
The moat becomes a street that curls
into a second circle
and a third, the tramways,
forms borders, then crosses them.
No. 11 carries everyone, briefly, together.
Die stad is vir iedereen, insists Wim.

The carriage sways around a building
and the city of Rubens and lace reveals itself.
"Kill cops" scrawls the graffiti
on modern brick next to old stone.

We pass the Hasidic neighborhood,
then the Moroccan one. Bakkerij Mustafa,
Auto Onderhoude, and Slagerei Nour in Dutch
and Arabic. A mother in a black scarf pushes a pram,
a boy running ahead wheeling his bicycle.

From the window, I see a florist pour
water from a bucket into the sloot,
a Madonna rounding the corner
of his building, and the cathedral above everything.

Water flows down the cobbled streets
toward the Schelde and the Rhine,
onward through Holland and Germany, giving
Rembrandt van Rijn his name, and the name
of my grandfather's cigarettes in Cape Town.

I follow the lines home
along the railway to Holland, and further,
to where the delta calls, and from there, open water
insistent as the birds, the seasons.

The port cities sing of other horizons.
Ships turn the curve of continents and the past
to islands on the other side of the world.

From the decks, the lights in the harbor
waver on the horizon.
From the shore, the ships dip
beneath the waves for eternities,
then rise again.

Languages string the docks together.
Leiden, city of suffering,
Cape Town, Camissa, place
of sweet water.

HANGKLIP*

I sink to the bodem
and the sea breathes me in,
swallows me down its long, blue throat.

I follow the almost-circle of the bay to Hangklip,
eye of a hook, past the black-purple shells
of akkrikels clinging to rocks in Kogelbaai.

Just beyond the jagged reef,
cormorants land with mournful caws
and claws scraping on rock,
their wings and sea-cries folding into quiet.

Now I am a sea snake
weaving close to the shore
through the pull and pulse of current.

Past the fishermen on Strandfontein casting
their long lines into the deep.
And past the empty shell of Monwabisi,
where children sink below the cruel waves.

Past the strand with no name
opposite Khayelitsha, "New Home."
And past the curve of road to Macassar, naming
the place across the ocean from which the slaves came.

Past the meridian of Seal Island, I follow
klipfish and sand sharks, shadows of pelicans
and gulls falling through the sky of water.

* Hangklip (Hanging Rock), on the far end of False Bay, was a place to which slaves in
the Cape Colony escaped.

And dolphins in their thousands accompany me
and whales are islands near me
and ships sail over memories.

Along the edge of the bay
the towns and rivers confess
their bare names for infinity,

Riviersonderend, river opening
on endlessness,
Kleinmond, small mouth opening
on endlessness,

washing against them,
the endlessness of memory.

Now I am one of the dead.
I pull myself to Hangklip on a cord of names.
I hear them sing in the throat of the sea,
the long, blue throat of the sea.

THE WORD

One day as a girl sitting
on the arm of my father's chair
where he settled after work
and we told each other our days
I spoke the word
used by the boy to give a name
to the thing he did that afternoon to my body
to the pain he said was a game

And that word
that word
in my mouth to my father
made him leap up straight
and shout to my mother at the sink
Did you hear what this child said

My mother is silent in my memory
but I learned from my father's fear
that the word I took from the boy
was a confession,
collusion, evidence that turned
my body into what it is,
and then
only then I knew the pain
could not be named
and so it became me

From the full span of his height
my father gazed down at my face,
trying to forget, trying
to reverse time
but history had heard us both
and couldn't go back

I sat there in the slow fall of light,
saying nothing
silent and static as what I believed was innocence
but still the word became my body

Afterward I hid
in my skin, in obedience, in an empty mouth
while the boy, the boy still lived opposite.
Sometimes the hot tar of the road
did not exist, as though their house heaved
right up against our windows,
his face at the glass,
so I stopped walking outside.

I skittered through novels unable
to bear the arc of women at risk
No one saves you like in the stories

I built myself a wall
and withdrew into its shadow
I pulled myself from my bones, leaving
them behind
I tore out the pages of my memory
so even the emptiness disappeared
I pared myself down
to the thinnest line, so much
like shelter did nothingness feel

Until one day I began to write
and I wrote until I could not forget
myself anymore
On the page appeared
each breath and gesture, each posture
of the body I had torn away
on the page appeared the years
and the words I could not speak
on the page appeared the pages

and the emptiness I had erased
on the page appeared my bones
and my memories
and at last I stepped again into my body.

NOT YOU

After nineteen years, I love
that you carry two books with you always,
The Poetry of Birds and the late
essays of John Berger. I love
that you read the same books over
and over, Pessoa's *The Book of Disquiet*,
and Yi-Fu's *Space and Place*, as though
visiting an infinite enigma. I love
that you love words seriously, that they matter
so much they make you angry and silent. I love
how you sit next to physicists and astronomers
and speak with them of infinity and they delight
then sadden you because their relation to numbers
holds no mystery. I love
how you tell me this, certain I know. I love
that you read me a poem each night
from the ones you've gathered all the years,
even if night is six hours apart and I'd rather face
the agony of your not-body.
Yes, I love that you love me, though
since the start I love you has been your way
to say goodnight, goodbye.
I love you, when you are tired
after two hours on Skype.
In the early days of the internet, when we loved
each other on dial-up, phoning
through the web in ten-minute segments
with aching two-second delays, I loved
that you were not a poem,
and you were, with your silences.
Right now, you are reading me the resistance of Rumi
to the limits of poetry and I'm still trying
to understand infinity.

Living in Cape Town in a three-year drought, I read
of people on other continents trapped
in a prison of rain, how it bends
them down with its opacity and scale,
and amid my compassion is envy
for what they are drowning in.
I think poetry is the flood
for the not-you I've prepared for
from the start.

I SAW YOU WALK TOWARD SOMETHING

for Keorapetse Kgositsile

You taught us that a border
is a place of yielding or refusing to yield,
for after refusal might lie a new country.
And the line runs through the land,
the mind, the skin. In all these,
you eluded capture, scaling
fences that scored you, left
a welt that marked the No
and the crossing.
Afterward, touching it, you knew,
this is the boundary.

You made a life of such crossings, and poetry,
a poetry of scar and soil and what troubled both.
In your writing and the way you looked at people,
the way you saw down to their bones,
you summoned a future before it existed,
and new musics on three continents,
every line inventing
and questioning its country.

And in freedom you drew poetry and music from others.
When we listened to you, we
who had stayed and we
who returned, did not divide ourselves
into our different losses but faced
the mutual hardness of making a country,
because you insisted on that hardness.

In the last days of a long year,
I saw you walk away,
slowly away, your right hand lifting
a little, your eyes drawn
to a place just ahead, as though toward
some strange welcome, as though toward
somewhere you already knew.

INTERVAL

Parsing my words in his office at the back
of the building, Archie Markham breathed in
and leaned toward me. Something is missing
from your poems—they need, he began
then halted, a stillness ringing
with movement. They need,
eyes creasing, head shaking back
and forth across a small span
. . . mmnhh . . .
the sound quick but not harsh,
his hands opening upward toward me,
chest tilted forward, spilling
out the breath of it, Not metaphors,
not images, but . . . mmnhh . . .
he who lived in words refused
a word, or words at all,
shoulders folding inward
around the necessary absence,
Not better ideas or forms, he insisted,
the quick compass of his gaze falling
on the breach at the heart of my lines, But life
and roughness and
. . . mmnhh . . . , he exhaled, half-rising
from his chair with the not-word.

Every gesture and jagged phatic
of that single hour of his long existence,
which began in Montserrat and took him
to Sheffield, Maputo, and Paris,
writing them all and the interval
between them,
is with me still.
Groundbreaker, you leapt

without scaffold.
That you leapt,
and sometimes fell,
revealed the interval
and what breathes there,
the ragged, the not-yet,
the core.

THE HISTORY OF INTIMACY

I.

You remember it because it's a wound.
A cut, twenty cuts, the name
for canings on the palm,
on the knuckles, on the buttocks,
a finely graded order of pain
that we who should not exist
were assigned for our failures.

II.

You keep you white, nuh,
Mike shouts in 1987 across the heads
of students sitting on Jameson Steps
and the sudden drawn silence shows
we are no longer in uniform in the quad
at Livingstone High, teasing, Hey,
why did you look through me
as though I don't exist. And this slipping
from being we called keeping you white,
but saying it out loud reveals
how we have learned
to measure our existence.

III.

In the video store after I've ordered a film,
my cousin elbows me, Why you putting on?
Putting on. Transitive verb. Putting on what?
Putting on skin, putting on
not-nothingness.

IV.

When the Group Areas Act is abolished,
my mother aches to go back
to the street she was removed from
and it is we, grown attached
to the scar we call home, who say, No,
we don't want to live in a white area,
this time ceding it ourselves.

V.

Mother, how do I write about you?
As a medical student on night duty,
you learned to sleep so lightly you could wake
in an instant in an emergency,

and for the rest of your life
your body became a body
that never again could sleep through the night.

You told of one evening when, for some reason
a little irked with my father, you left the table early,
returning to the bedroom by yourself,
and found my sister blue for lack of breath.
To this day, you recall what anger gave you,
how it saved my sister's life. Anger. Breath.

Since the beginning, you have been breath,
and poetry.

You told me how Black students were asked
to leave the room during the autopsy of white bodies.
And of my writing about this, you said,
That is my story. That is not your story.
And now, with the illness you could not speak of for years,
Mother, am I once again turning your words
and your silence into a poem?

VI.

In 1988 at Crawford train station, my brother and I find
a blue plank hand-painted in yellow letters:
"Non-Whites Only" on one side,
"Whites Only" on the other,
thrown away by the fence next to the tracks.
Picking it up, we see the two sides
of the sign lay back-to-back,
each half resting against its opposite,
intimate and inverse
but unknown to each other.

We knew this was history
someone had made by hand, then hidden
and tried to forget. We bring it home
and come across it sometimes in a corner
when we're looking for something else.

ANSWERING

It's 1991. With two degrees and no job, I'm called
for an interview: secretary's position
at a small law firm in Claremont. Two men question me,
one older, his jacket off, sleeves rolled up
and a nervous flush to his face; the other younger,
quiet, buttoned-up. Paging through my CV,
the older man tilts his head and asks,
What did you learn
at the pinko-liberal place on the hill
you can use in the real world? I blame
Mandela's release and the formlessness of the time
for actually talking about changing the economy.
He sighs and retorts, Please, tell me something
you didn't hear in a lecture, something
that surprises me, something
not just politically correct. For instance,
the younger man takes his turn, reaching
into himself for a piece of the real, I can't stand
the way, when the robot is red, Black women walk
across the pedestrian crossing as though
they have all the time in the world.
I sometimes think of what he sees, stalled
at the light, metal drumming
beneath his feet, as a woman cuts
across the world, answering
only to herself.

THE LAW OF THE MOTHER

You and your sisters ask your mother if it hurts on your wedding night when your hymen is broken and she answers, It's a membrane and it doesn't break, just gets nudged aside, and it doesn't hurt if you're gentle with each other and take your time.

On hearing this, you are puzzled because everyone tells you the breaking is the sign of a good woman, but you grasp that she has told you the law of the mother.

One day when you are five, a boy in the neighborhood says, Let's play Mummy and Daddy, and when it hurts, he warns you not to say anything to your parents.

And you tell your father
and the world fissures.
And who do you turn to then?

To shame, an internal script you learned
before the sin, and rehearse again and again.

Virgin. Fallen.

You are sentenced to your body, your
bitter body, your memory.

For months you forget, then in the middle of class shame jolts through every vein in your body, driving the breath from you. This becomes such a pattern, you realize the aftermath of hurt is its own form.

Sex is both impossible and the only way to be modern. How can you be a Muslim feminist when you're a virgin lying about sex to your friends?

One night, talking with your sisters in the dark, you vow: If anyone ever hurts you, come tell me and I promise I'll stand with you. And as you say this, the scene where Thelma works out why Louise left Texas and never went back replays in your mind, and you understand for the first time:

It happened to you too, didn't it?

And even on the desperate race from the police to freedom in Mexico, Louise refuses to drive the direct route through Texas, to go back there and let any part of it touch her again.

You think therapy is for white people till you confide in a lecturer who wrote about rape and she tells you to come back, and you do for an hour each Friday for a year, till you ask with a ragged throat,

if everything you are
was born of that breaking,
is a subset of breaking,
is broken

She, deep-souled lesbian woman, tells you

that "broken" is a boundary
and the body is time
as well as place.

And with this, with this,
you permit yourself to return
to what happened, to where

you shed your bones and flesh,
and self threads into its casing,
enters again each knot and hollow.

CARDINAL POINTS

Louise and I hurtle down the M5
in my blue tjorrie, beating the evening rush
to Kalk Bay for the end-of-year party
at Jane and David's place

We coil around Sunrise Circle
stop by Muizenberg
peel off our clothes
and dive through phosphorescence

our hair a meniscus
at sunset
at the shore
at the end of light

Another world clings to us
when we arrive at the party
and Chris says
your long, wet hair and your
bodies bearing the sea and he says
nothing else, already too much

I look back at that night
halfway and perpetual
and we are swimming out further
into the Southern Ocean
untethered to time

where gravity's centrifuge
makes us south and east
and all the cardinal points

our five-angled figures turning
to the earth's commands, floating

on breath
and reflection
and the body's physics

night endless
in all directions

akkrikels   periwinkles (Afrikaans)

angel of history   a figure described by German critic Walter Benjamin in reference to Paul Klee's 1920 print *Angelus Novus*: an angel whose wings carry it into the future while its head remains turned toward the past

Athlone   one of many Black townships on the Cape Flats, a sprawling, sandy area in the lee of Table Mountain. Generally, the Flats are a less desirable part of Cape Town, but Athlone is an old suburb (some houses date to the nineteenth century) with a mix of working-class and middle-class residents.

Black   spelled with an uppercase B in the South African sense, it signals a unified political identity that refutes the divisions of apartheid racial categories—such as Bantu, Indian, and Coloured—and the negation of Non-White. *See* Coloured

bodem   seabed (Afrikaans)

Camissa   "Place of sweet water," the Khoi name for the site where Cape Town was established

Cape Colony   the area of colonial settlement by the Dutch: Cape Town generally and the whole area around the Cape of Good Hope. A brutal slaveholding system shaped the society and economy of the Colony from 1658, six years after the Dutch established a settlement at the Cape, until 1834, when the British abolished slavery throughout the empire.

Coloured   a racial category in South Africa established under a foundational apartheid law, the Population Registration Act of 1950, which decreed that "A Coloured is a person who is not a White person or a Bantu [the racist apartheid term for 'Black' or 'African']."

Daai is maar doenya se goete   "These are merely earthly matters" (Afrikaans, though "doenya" is from the Arabic word for "earth" or "near")

Die stad is vir iedereen   "This city is for everyone" (Vlaams/Dutch)

doek a scarf used as a head covering (Afrikaans but now part of South African English)

Epilogue the last program of the night on South African TV in the apartheid era, a Christian prayer

Flats the Cape Flats, an extensive, low-lying area to which Black people in Cape Town were removed from the 1960s onward. Townships on the Cape Flats were thus framed by loss at first, but they were also the only home known to the children of those removed, like me—so the area holds multiple meanings. *See* Athlone; Group Areas Act; removed

Florence Florence "Flo" Mtoba (1966–2001), a prominent manager in the South African music industry and an arts administrator in Gauteng Province. She was married to the jazz pianist Moses Molelekwa and was also his manager. Mtoba died by strangulation on February 13, 2001, apparently at the hands of her husband. *See* Moses.

Frans Masereel (1889–1972) a Belgian printmaker and graphic artist. I had a brief writer's residency at the Frans Masereel Centre just outside Antwerp and was mesmerized by his scenes of the city at night.

Group Areas Act (1950) one of apartheid's most destructive laws, which decreed that residential areas should be racially segregated, a policy carried out through the "forced removal" of Black people from mixed neighborhoods to deprived areas far from urban centers.

gudri a homemade bed covering constructed by quilting old sheets and fabric scraps together

helm caul, as in "born with a caul" (Afrikaans)

ID book the government-issued identity documents bound in distinctive green covers that South Africans carry with them everywhere. Today, such documents serve bureaucratic functions and are used to secure a job and open a bank account, but they are also shadowed by the memory of the infamous passbooks that Black people were forced to carry during apartheid, on pain of arrest, and that were used to exile people within their own country. The ID photos enclosed in the familiar green binding still have a haunted quality to me.

ja yes (Afrikaans)

Jameson Steps   the steps below the central hall at the University of Cape Town. Both the steps and hall were named after an ally of Cecil John Rhodes, Leander Starr Jameson, who led a failed raid on the Transvaal Republic in 1895. After the #RhodesMustFall student protests of 2015, Jameson Hall was renamed Sarah Baartman Hall, for the Khoi woman taken to Europe in 1810 and exhibited as the "Hottentot Venus." Her remains were returned to South Africa in 2002 and given an official burial.

Keorapetse Kgositsile (1938–2018)   a South African poet, teacher, and anti-apartheid activist who lived in exile for three decades in the United States and in countries around the African continent before returning to South Africa in 1990. He was appointed as the country's National Poet Laureate in 2006 and famously nurtured the work of younger writers.

Khayelitsha   "New Home" (Xhosa), a large township for Black people established in 1983 by the apartheid government, located far from the center of Cape Town and still largely impoverished and marked by informal housing

klipfish   a group of small, brightly colored fish found around the South African coast

kloof   a steep ravine in the mountains

Kwikspar   a mini-mart chain in South Africa

marabi   a style of rapid jazz that developed in South African townships in the 1930s and became the foundation of musical forms including mbaqanga and kwela

Monk   Thelonious Sphere Monk (1917–1982), a virtuoso American jazz pianist and composer known for his improvisational style

Monwabisi   "Bringing Joy" (Xhosa), a beach facility created by the apartheid government for Black people. Such facilities were always located in the less desirable and more dangerous areas of the coast, and drownings were tragically common.

Moses Moses Taiwa Molelekwa (1973–2001), a South African jazz prodigy whose music reshaped the language of jazz in South Africa. His albums also looked outward toward the rest of the continent and the diaspora. When Molelekwa died, apparently by suicide, he was found next to the body of his wife, Florence Mtoba, who had been strangled.

nuh no (Afrikaans, colloquial)

removed evokes the policy of "forced removals" of Black people from their homes and neighborhoods. *See* Group Areas Act

robot South African term for "traffic light"

rockery rock garden

sloot gutter (Afrikaans, but also used in English)

Strandfontein "Beach Fountain" (Afrikaans), an area on the coast of the Cape of Good Hope far from Cape Town, established by the apartheid government for the use of "Coloured" people

Thelma & Louise (1991) an American film written by Callie Khouri and directed by Ridley Scott; a feminist touchstone in cinema. At a crucial moment in the narrative, Thelma (played by Geena Davis) discovers that Louise (portrayed by Susan Sarandon) had been raped when she lived in Texas.

tjorrie a jalopy or old, beaten-up car (South African English, colloquial)

VW vernacular shorthand for Volkswagen

wattle a tree imported from Australia that now grows prodigiously around the Cape; also called a Port Jackson. "Port Jackson, Cape Town" alludes to an infamous series of murders of twenty-two boys, some of whom were found buried in shallow graves under dense wattle growth.

white spelled with a lowercase "w" to refuse the centrality, fixity, and racism with which apartheid imbued whiteness

ACKNOWLEDGMENTS

Keorapetse Kgositsile, living inspiration and now ancestor; Harry Garuba,
I hear your breath in each line; Ingrid Fiske, lodestar; Pumla Gqola, for
the honor of the Wits Humanities Writer in Residence fellowship (and
everything you mean to me); Jane Bennett, for listening at the beginning;
Sean O'Toole, for the invitation to write a piece for *Art South Africa,* from
which emerged the title of this collection; the DaimlerChrysler Award, for
the collection *The Museum of Ordinary Life,* in which "Closer" appeared;
James Woodhouse, who invited me to write a new book of poetry in which
to republish "Closer"; the Academic and Non-Fiction Authors' Association
of South Africa, for their support at a crucial stage; the Humanities Institute
at Penn State; my beloved departments: Women's, Gender, and Sexuality
Studies and African Studies at Penn State and the English Department at
Stellenbosch University; the Dr. Sisters; my dear friends from International
Poetry Nights in Hong Kong; the brilliant board members of the African
Poetry Book Fund, with whom I am lucky to serve; my brother poets Kwame
Dawes and Matthew Shenoda for recommending my work to Parneshia
Jones; my sister poets, Patricia Jabbeh Wesley, TJ Dema, Tsitsi Jaji, and
Abena Busia, to whom I confided earlier versions of some of these poems;
Civitella Ranieri Foundation, for a generative writing fellowship; Veerle
Rooms, Wim Persoon, Charl-Pierre Naudé, and E-Pos; the pure delight of
bringing out a book with Kwela and now Northwestern University Press,
with particular thanks to Parneshia, Maia, Robin, Marianne, Patrick, JD,
Olivia, and Anne; Rustum Kozain, whose editor's eye vastly improved these
poems; Carolyn Meads, for a year of tea and translation in Stellenbosch and
for hours of working together on the manuscript; Shaida Kazie Ali, who
teaches me what writing can do; my eternal muse, Louise Green; my brother,
Imran Jardine, a walking poem; the nineties; for those who are inside;
Jonathan Marks, for sharing his exquisite eye as a photographer and writer;
my teachers Gabe Welsch, Archie Markham, Kim Welsch, Sean O'Brien,
and Robin Becker; Julia Kasdorf, poetic inspiration, for the invitation to
read at the beautiful Bellefonte Art Museum; Lisa Sternlieb, for tessellation,
and Chris Staley, for densities, at Han Wingate and Russell Frank's poetry
evening; the organizers and students at the 2017 Poetry Festival at Nelson

Mandela University; for their subtle and poetic sense of language, my thanks to the brilliant and generous polyglots who worked on the translations in "Everything We've Said": Anna Ziajka Stanton, Jon Brockopp, Samar Farage, Maha Marouan, Joan Landes, Bénédicte Monicat, Shahid Mathee, Abdulkader Tayob, Omaima Abu-Bakr, Loyiso Mletshe, JC (Oom Koos) Oosthuysen, and Thokozile Mabeqa; Marty Camden, for crafting the glorious cover of the Kwela edition and shaping this one; my golden Franckie, Peso, and Orleans; and the Stellenbosch Institute for Advanced Study, in whose exquisite setting and company this book came to fruition. My mother and my father, my beginning, to whom I return again and again. And you, Slow Fall of Light.

CREDITS

Some of the poems have appeared in earlier versions in the following venues:

"Closer" (as "I Used to Live"): *Meridians: Feminism, Race, Transnationalism* 5, no. 2 (2005): 84.

"Closer" (as "I Used to Live"): Gabeba Baderoon, *The Museum of Ordinary Life*, chapbook (Stuttgart: DaimlerChrysler, 2005).

"Rain Falls on the Abstract World": *Revolver 133, E-Pos II* 33, no. 4 (March 2007): 18.

"The Port Cities": *St. Petersburg Review* 2 (2008): 62–63.

"A Prospect of Beauty and Unjustness": *World Literature Today* 82, no. 4 (Jul./Aug. 2008): 12.

"Concentration": *Kunapipi* 34, no. 1 (2012): 117–23.

"Axis and Revolution": *The Common* 4 (Oct. 2012): 181–82.

"Effective Immediately": *Harvard Divinity Bulletin* 41, nos. 3–4 (Summer/ Autumn 2013).

"The Flats": *Cultural Studies* 27, no. 3 (2013): 482–86.

"Song of the Husband 2" and "Everything We've Said" (as "Language Poems"): *Journal for Islamic Studies* 33 (2013): 201–2.

"Focal Length," "Poetry for Beginners," and "Tell Me What You See" (as "ID Photos"): *Feminist Studies* 41, no. 1 (2015): 134 –37.

"Surface," "The Edges of Things" (as "Highway Fox"), and "Kogelbaai" (as "Koggelbaai"): *New Contrast*, no. 179 (Spring 2017).

"Hangklip": *Illuminations* 32 (2017).

"Poetry for Beginners," "Tell Me What You See" (as "ID Photos"), and "A Prospect of Beauty" (as "The Prospect of Beauty and Unjustness"): Gabeba Baderoon, *Poetry for Beginners*, chapbook (Hong Kong: Chinese University of Hong Kong, 2017).

"I saw you walk toward something": *Odd Magazine*, 2018.

"Not You": *New Coin* 54, no. 1 (June 2018): 9–10.

"Promised Land": *Johannesburg Review of Books*, June 4, 2018.

"The History of Intimacy," "Interval," and "Ghost Technologies": *WritingThreeSixty* 4, no. 1 (2018): 146–50.

"Green Pincushion Proteas": Academy of American Poets Poem-a-Day, August 6, 2018.

"The Word": *Feminism Is: South Africans Speak Their Truth*, ed. Jen Thorpe, Vlaeberg: Kwela, 2018.

My thanks to the editors.